The Three Way Tavern

D0250293

The publisher gratefully acknowledges the generous contributions to this book provided by Lannan Foundation, by the Sunshik Min Endowment for the Advancement of Korean Literature at the Korea Institute, Harvard University, and by the Daesan Foundation.

Translated with a generous grant from the Daesan Foundation.

The Three Way Tavern

SELECTED POEMS

KO UN

TRANSLATIONS BY CLARE YOU
AND RICHARD SILBERG

FOREWORD BY GARY SNYDER

UNIVERSITY OF CALIFORNIA PRESS

BERKELEY LOS ANGELES LONDON

University of California Press, one of the most distinguished
university presses in the United States, enriches lives around
the world by advancing scholarship in the humanities, social
sciences, and natural sciences. Its activities are supported by
the UC Press Foundation and by philanthropic contributions
from individuals and institutions. For more information,
visit www.ucpress.edu.

University of California Press
Berkeley and Los Angeles, California

University of California Press, Ltd.
London, England

Some earlier versions of these translations and of the intro-
duction appeared in various issues of the magazine *Korean
Culture*. Some of these translations appeared in *Parthenon
West Review*, no. 3 (Fall 2005).

© 2006 by The Regents of the University of California

Library of Congress Cataloging-in-Publication Data

Ko, Un, 1933–.
    The three way tavern : selected poems / Ko Un ; foreword
by Gary Snyder ; translations by Clare You and Richard
Silberg.
        p.   cm.
    Includes bibliographical references.
    ISBN 0-520-24612-8 (cloth : alk. paper)
    ISBN 0-520-24613-6 (pbk. : alk. paper)
    I. You, Clare.   II. Silberg, Richard, 1942–.   III. Title.
PL992.42.U5A2   2006
895.7'14—dc22   2005031020

Manufactured in Canada

14   13   12   11   10   09   08   07   06
10   9   8   7   6   5   4   3   2   1

The paper used in this publication meets the minimum
requirements of ANSI/NISO Z39.48–1992 (R 1997)
(*Permanence of Paper*).

In memory of Dr. Youngbin "Y.B." Yim

Contents

FROM A Cenotaph (1997)

FROM **Ten Thousand Lives** (1986–)

FROM **Ko Un's Sŏn Poems: What?** (1991)

Foreword

One afternoon in the late 1990s, Ko Un and I read poems together to a small audience in Northern California. Friends had gotten us together, of an age to be brothers and each with a quirky take on the world, living on opposite sides of the big ocean. I read his poems in English with a bold out-loud voice and then he read them in Korean, his voice almost a whisper, sharpening people's ears and making us all alert. His otherworldly voice made the poems even more powerful. That was my first lesson, of many, from Ko Un.

Korea is the less-known country between China and Japan that partakes of both cultures and does their high styles extremely well, but also keeps its own archaic heritage with all its difference: stubborn and strong, proud, elegant, gritty, bold, and deeply conservative. A people descended from the Bear-mother (who gave birth to King Tan'gun); a high civilization where women shamans play a role in religious life. In the Buddhist mountain monasteries, nominally Sŏn (or, in Japanese, Zen), they still engage with the "Flower Wreath Sutra," Queen of Sutras, almost forgotten everywhere else in the world. Ko Un retold in Korean a chunk of this sutra—known as *Hua Yen* in Chinese, *Kegon* in Japanese, *Hwaŏm* in Korean—and it became a best seller. Korea honors a Confucian practice older and purer than whatever's left in China or Japan. There are lots of zealous Christian converts and plenty of well-read socialists and unionists in Korea. And there's always a crew of hard-drinking politicians (as well as poets and artists), and sharpie-dressed women. Korea has great food (not too hot at all) and restaurants, each with its own crock of rice beer bubbling, and giant vats of various types of kimchee pickles that bubble too.

The traditional poems of China and Japan are not so alike. Korea's poetry too has qualities all its own. The languages each have their own specifics, and the writing systems, though related, are now far apart. Ko Un's poetry in modern Korean is different again, though still clearly within the East Asian mold. Because of their purity, their nervy clarity, and their heart of compassion, his poems are not only "Korean"—they belong to the world.

This book is a selection from the many volumes of poems Ko Un has written—out of day's work and human turmoil and delight in the countless little towns and farms on Planet Earth. Ko Un's poems evoke the open creativity and fluidity of nature, and the funny turns and twists of Mind. Mind is sometimes registered in Buddhist terms—Buddhist practice being part of Ko Un's background. Ko Un writes spare, short-line lyrics direct to the point, but often intricate in both wit and meaning. There are also a few long poetic meditations. He writes particular poems of people's lives: one of his projects is to do ten thousand poems for ten thousand different persons; some of those are gathered here.

I savor his play between the Pure Land (a Buddhist vision) in the poem "Hometown"—

> If you go back before you were a man,
> that's where your home is.
> No, not even there, go back further.
>
> Just try yelling without yearning
> in the simple voice of an animal
> what the beast returns to,
> the pure land, that's home.

—and the—what shall I call it?—"Toxic Land," a modern vision, a trickster "pure land," in the poem "Back Home":

I came back
to where trash
blooms like flowers—
this is the world I longed for.

There's a poem called "Letters" that tells of a day in grade school during the Pacific War and the teacher asking the children what or who would they like to be. Ko Un responded, "Emperor" (of Japan). This was a great scandal, and after being banned three months from school, he was asked the question again. He said, "A mailman."

I wanted to be a man who delivers messages from one man to another.
I loved the mailman and the mail.
When the mail bike showed up, I closed my books and trotted after it,
though no letters came for me.
Twenty pieces of mail are all the village gets a year.

A lot of the American interest in Ko Un came through the buzz of Zen (Sŏn) and his 1997 booklet *Beyond Self,* with a fine foreword written by Allen Ginsberg. Some of those small verses are included here, in the section from *Ko Un's Sŏn Poems: What?* and they are koan-like kernels of deep dharma wit. Yet he is not simply a Zen poet. His earlier book *Sound of My Waves* (1993) has many poems of people's daily country and small-town life, hands- and feet-on. It is a further challenge to get to know this post-Zen side of Ko Un and his later complexly situated, totally contemporary poetic view.

Ko Un has lived through many of the lives his poems embody. Peasant village boy, bright student, army conscript, Sŏn monk for ten years, schoolteacher, writer, published convivial poet-drinker, political activist for greater South Korean democracy, fiction writer, political prisoner, family man, and major public cultural figure—there's even a movie made from his epic based on the "Flower Wreath Sutra," *Little Pilgrim!*

Our totem fish and indicator species for the whole North Pacific Rim, around the Aleutian chain from Korea to the Big Sur River, is salmon. So then, what about a rowdy peasant marriage festival—

Salmon

So sleek and so handsome
she swam away to a distant sea,
with a normal gray back and
a silvery white belly,
lived four glorious years in the sea.

Empty body without food.
Beautiful body,
the head swells,
its mouth hooks,
ugly as can be,
red dots swarming her.

I can't look at
her ugliness.
When the ugly woman
heads straight home

the world lights up.
From far away
you can hear the party drums beat.

Even though he stays specific with mustard flowers and barley, with names of hills and provinces, Ko Un has now traveled worldwide and is not only a major spokesperson for all of Korean culture, but a voice for Planet Earth Watershed as well.

Gary Snyder
First Month 2005

Introduction

Ko Un, poet, novelist, literary critic, political dissident, and ex-Buddhist monk, among many other things, is often called *keobong* (a great mountain peak) by his peers. It seems a fair metaphor, not only because of the enormous volume of work he has produced, but also for its content. It resonates with the same awe-invoking mythic power that a great mountain has, a great mountain with its deep valleys and peaks and varied and abundant wildlife, ranging from ancient towering trees to tiny delicate flowers and from the beast of prey to the minute insect.

Ko Un is unquestionably a giant among contemporary Korean poets. His poetry is filled with memories and experiences, ranging from those of his childhood to those of the senior man he now is, having passed that important milestone of life, the *ch'ilsoon* (seventieth birthday); he has lived as a precocious boy, a soul-searching monk, a tormented, nihilistic vagabond, a vitriolic dissident, and, finally, a family man.

Although he is not yet widely known in the United States, he has been succinctly described by Allen Ginsberg (in his foreword to Ko Un's *Beyond Self*): "Ko Un is a magnificent poet, a combination of Buddhist cognoscente, passionate political libertarian, and naturalist historian."[1]

HIS LIFE

Born Ko Un-Tae in 1933 in a small village near Kunsan in North Chulla Province, Ko Un early served notice that he was not going to be an obedient son. Although he excelled in his schoolwork, he was a pale, sickly child who brashly claimed that he wished to be emperor, an aspiration for which he was quickly and severely reprimanded by his Japanese schoolmaster. He later wrote about the incident in the poems "Letters" and "Headmaster Abé." This incident was his first experience with oppression, as a subjugated citizen under Japanese rule. Oppressive events such as this led him to one of his enduring themes, the denial of the human rights of the Korean people.

Born to a farming family, Ko Un came from humble origins, yet he had a nurturing home environment; he had a maternal grandmother whose love for him was absolute, and he grew up with a father who, after a long day of toil, kept the lamp burning late into the night to read storybooks, which helped him to forget his fatigue and poverty. His uncles owned books that Ko Un enjoyed reading, and he studied the Chinese classics at an early age. This traditional rural life was not to last for long, however, either for him or for other children his age, as the ravages of the Korean War reached into his village and into his life. As a teenager, he witnessed the ultimate human cruelty, that of killing and being killed, among his family, his friends, and his neighbors, for causes unclear to him. He had to turn helplessly away from a friend's plea for rescue from imminent death. He stood powerless as his uncles and cousins were led away to be shot.

These suffocating events hounded his dreams. He was restless; forsaking school, he roamed the countryside, making long forays into the neighboring hills, seeking to cure his despondency. Then he left home, embarking on a long journey of aimless wandering and many hardships. To make a living, he joined a street gang of taffy vendors; he was even briefly jailed on the charge of being a suspicious character. Subsequent events led him to a meeting with the Buddhist monk Hyech'o, and he entered the

Buddhist community; in 1952, he became a disciple of the Venerable Hyobong. For the next ten years, he lived the life of a Sŏn (Zen) Buddhist monk, studying and meditating in the Sŏn tradition.

Although as a youth he had felt a vague desire to be a painter, in his later years Ko Un was attracted to the company of writers and poets and intellectuals. While he was a monk, he wrote and edited the abbot's dharma talks, started a newspaper for the Buddhist community, and wrote poems. His first collection of poems, *Feelings of Paramita,* written mostly in the Heinsa Temple, was published in 1960. Being a monk requires discipline and a lifetime commitment, but Ko Un's temperament was too passionate and his ties to the secular life too strong for him to detach himself completely from the world. One spring day, as he wrote in his 1993 autobiography, *Na* (I), things came to a head while he was in meditation with Master Hyobong. As hard as he tried to hang on to the *hwadu* (the meditation topics, or koans), the devil would appear within him, kicking the *hwadu,* one by one, out of his mind. Youthful lust and desire overpowered him. He could hear the floor squeak as his master left to go to the bathroom. He said to himself, "I can't stand it any longer. What's the Buddha for, anyway! A howling doubt overtook me from inside, the rage exploded." He ran out the door, grabbed an ax, and slammed it down onto the squeaky floor. The floor split. He yelled, "Master, what's the use of becoming a Buddha!" To his surprise, Master Hyobong responded, "You're right. What's the use. Let's quit. Let's quit . . . and just have fun," and the master dropped to the floor and lay down, stretching out his legs. The youthful disciple knelt in shame, and, together, they continued the meditation. The master, however, must have foreseen what was to become of Ko Un, for he said to him later in the day, as Ko was tending the fire for the *ondol* floor, "There are only flames within you. The flames, will they be gone after the body is completely consumed! Oh my, my." Ko Un holds Master Hyobong's teachings dear to his heart to this very day.

Ko Un left the Buddhist community in 1963 with the essay "Hwansok" (Returning to Secular Life), which was published in *Hankuk-ilbo* newspaper. He decided it was time for him to choose between religion and literature. In the old world, he reasoned, religion and literature were one. If so, his poems should reflect the religious part of him, and his religion would serve as an infinite energy source for his writings. Unfortunately for him, they could not be reconciled; the schism between his religion and the literature of the modern world was, for him, too great.

While leaving the religious community was an honest choice for him, he wrote that he saw it as a cowardly act. When he left the temple, some friends in the Buddhist community rejected him outright, saying, "Ko Un is no longer! Ko Un is dead," and some greeted him with a smile and said, "Now you really are Wonhyo!"[2] He could stand the cold rejections better than the pleasant greetings; he felt deeply ashamed.

He was once again becoming despondent, and facing the real world was difficult. It led him back to nihilistic depression and insomnia. For the next three years, until 1966, he taught at a charitable school for children on Cheju Island. He read much and wrote many poems, essays, and novels in this period but was still in torment. He has said that during this time he was never completely free of the same despair he had felt in the 1950s.[3]

An abrupt turn in his life came in the early winter of 1970, when he picked up an old piece of newspaper from a tavern floor. He read a short human-interest article about the suicide by self-immolation of a poor laborer. In later years, he recalled: "Indeed, the death of Jun Taeil was the source of the strength that pulled me from the deepest abyss of my life. . . . After leaving Hyobong, I gladly joined Jun Taeil's cause. . . . Now I was already thrown into the rough sea of history and I eagerly swam on its waves with a passion. I had no hesitation about dashing into a flame or into deep water."[4] With this passion, he took upon himself the cause of civil rights. He became a militant activist poet and the leader in the *minjung munhak* (people's literature) movement. His activities caused him to be jailed by the military regime then in power, but his poems, which reflected the desires and sentiments of the people, were enormously popular. Throughout his jail experience, although it was painful, he was inspired to record in his poetry the lives of ordinary people; he wanted to celebrate through poetry each and every life he encountered, no matter how insignificant, for now all life was precious to him. The lives he recorded in this fashion appeared in the volumes of the work-in-progress *Ten Thousand Lives* (1986–). In his jail cell, he also resolved to record, in *Paektu Mountain* (1987–94),[5] the saga of the Korean freedom fighters under Japanese colonial rule.

There were those who severely criticized Ko Un for his political activities, who believed that being involved in politics and being militant were not in a "true poet's" character; critics who believed in "art for art's sake" had no use for poets like Ko Un. Other critics said that "people's literature" was not a new genre thought up by Ko Un and his followers; it had always existed.

Another big change came into Ko Un's life in 1983: at the age of fifty, he ended his long solitary life by getting married. He settled in a rural town a couple of hours away from the urban sprawl of Seoul. As the government became more democratic and the civil unrest of the working people subsided, his poems became more reflective of past events, but they continued to display those elements of realism combined with a Sŏn spirituality that had always characterized his poetry.

When asked what he would say to the new generation of poets, Ko Un responds that he believes his future is cast in with theirs; in a sense, he is in love with them. Yet because there are few whom he could count as influences among the literary men of the recent past, his outlook on the future leans darkly toward uncertainty: "Today's young poets are too indifferent to the ultimate anguish of mankind. I hope you, young people, will experience bankruptcy, dedication, madness, mental anguish, and so on. I also ask this of myself. When I say 'You!' it also refers to 'I,' embracing you and me as one, wishing to stand apart from selfishness." He adds, "'I didn't come here to learn, I came to be drunk,' I also love to drink. We must sometimes become foolish by drinking."[6]

His love of drinking lays bare his sense of humor. Once he and a drinking buddy were on a lecture trip to a Buddhist temple. As usual, his friend needed a drink and invited Ko Un to join him. To his surprise, Ko Un vehemently declined. The friend's devilish nature could not let Ko Un be. As he prodded and urged him to join in, Ko Un pulled out from under his shirt a string with a small piece of paper attached to it and said, "See this?" Ko Un's face was serious as his friend craned his neck to read the two characters, "NO DRINK." Ko Un put the string and paper back where it had been put by his young wife; he put it away like an innocent child putting away a shaman's potent amulet. That night, however, they were very drunk.[7]

A man of wantonness and spiritual yearning, with outbursts of creative energy, an irrepressible distaste for oppressors, an insatiable appetite for the unknown, a wry sense of humor—this seems to describe the temperament of Ko Un.

Ko Un and his wife—they have one daughter studying abroad—now live in Majung village, where "Children throw stones. . . . pheasants flutter away, frightened for no reason."[8] He rises early every day, writes till noon, takes a walk before he resumes writing, writes until dinner, and reads for the rest of the day.

He is a well-established poet, revered by many and criticized by some; he does not look like a moon-faced Buddha or an absentminded scholar; he is lean, keen, and spry. He may yet turn another page in his life.

HIS POEMS

Ko Un has authored more than one hundred volumes of poems, long and short fiction, essays, literary critiques, and children's stories. Many have been best sellers, with a large following of avid readers. About his immense output of work, he says: "I believe in diligence as a writer. Maybe you can call that a 'passion for *sirhak* (practical learning).' No matter, this attitude makes me put out a fair amount of writing and crisscross among genres, in the process expanding the limits of each. I am a restless man, restless by nature. Not only am I restless in the twilight of the sunset and in the moonlight, I must cry in them like the birds and the beasts. I have to cry. This must have contributed to the large volume of my work."⁹

His prose poems range from Basho-like verses of a couple of lines to a Homeric epic of thousands of lines; his themes range from a minuscule insect to the vastness of ten thousand human lives, and from a simple observation to the most profound spirituality. His restless body and soul are endlessly seeking the meaning of life. His forty-five years of poetry reflect the history of his life, his personal journey, both emotional and philosophical.

Ko Un's works are generally divided into three stages: the first period, of "nihilistic wantonness"; the second period, of "resistance activism" or "social responsibility"; and the third period, the poetic culmination of his artistry, of "the language of ordinary people."

The early poems, consisting of the volumes *Feelings of Paramita* (1960), *Seaside Verses* (1966), and *God Is the Last Village of Words* (1967), mirror his restless wandering. They speak of shadowy death in its coffin; sad illness, as in "Lavishness" or "Consumption"; the doomed heart, as in "The Heart of a Poet"; and the futility of life, as in "Praxis and Break," in which he sings of the death of his younger brother, whose "heart and body are cleansed pure":

> Each story the dead told my brother
> was preserved, dried in the sun.
> Truly this world is the same as
> that other big world of the graves.
> Starting tomorrow, let's not send away visitors; let's live together.

In the early years, despite emotional struggle and the instability that swirled around him, there was always a Sŏn spirituality running through his poems, as in "The Rhyme of Ch'on-un Temple," "Feelings of a Mountain Temple," and even "Bug's Trill" and "Spring Rain."

The second stage of his literary work began in 1974 with the publication of *Gone to Munui Village*, followed by *Into the Mountain Quiet* (1977), *Dawn's Road* (1978), *Stars of Home* (1984), and many more. One laborer's tragic death left an indelible mark on his life, as noted earlier; he took up the cause of the oppressed and developed a strong sense of social responsibility. He became a militant poet, meeting authority with the rash daring of a moth flying into a flame, as evoked in the poems in *Gone to Munui Village*.

In "Casting a Net," he laments the tragic history of his people,

> No grief is left for me now.
> Grief kept me going, not luck,
> there was no other way.

and goes on to castigate the oppressors:

> The disasters were fiercer than dragons.
> I cast a net on the wide East Sea
> and spread my catch on the beaches to dry like squid.
>
> Masters of the peninsula, don't auction off this grief
> whatever the price!
> Not this grief, drying glittery as my squid.
> No! No!

In "Killing Life," he wants the old, corrupt, foul social order to be destroyed and a new order started:

Mow down parents and children.
This, that, and the others,
everything else.
Knife them in the dark.
Next morning
the world is piled with death.
Our chore is burying them all day

and building a new world on it.

His stand for the common people was forged from his sense of history—a history steeped in suffering caused by oppression, inequality, and fratricidal struggle. His early passive stance was later transformed into an active urging of others to join him.

In "Arrow," from *Dawn's Road,* he challenges people to transform themselves into arrows, "throwing away like rage" all we have accumulated and enjoyed for decades in exchange for a fair and just world. In its ending, one can hear the echoes of distant warriors battling:

The air's whole body shrieks;
let's go
piercing through the air!
The target rushes in at dark noon.
The target, gushing blood, falls at last;
this once
let's all bleed as arrows!

No coming back!
No coming back!

Ah, arrows! Arrows of our country! Our warriors! The warriors' souls!

When his *Pastoral Poems* came out in 1986, Ko Un had a comfortable home, having ended fifty years of solitude and having settled with his new wife in a rural town. *O Poems, Fly Away!* (1986), *Your Eyes* (1988), *Morning Dew* (1990), the ongoing *Ten Thousand Lives,* and many more poems followed. Although his poems were vividly original and protean in style, they were steeped in Sŏnesque ideals; they were passionate, impregnated with realism, and at the same time filled with the sense of ultimate emptiness that pervades all his work.

In *Paektu Mountain,* such is the poet's creative energy that, with his fierce, burning love for the lives and history of the people, his epic poem spins out over fifty thousand lines, telling the Korean people's struggle for independence from Japan. While evoking a time and place unfamiliar to most of us, it tells the story of a defiant couple caught in the tragedy of Korean history. The poem begins with a young farmhand and his master's only daughter fleeing north for love, freedom, and a new life. It follows their lives for forty years, from 1900 to 1940, until five years before the liberation of Korea. The saga begins:

Prelude

Oh, the eternal gales
sweeping through the valleys of Changkun Summit and Mangch'unhu,
Oh, the gusty winds no one can tame,

these are the sons and sons of sons of Korea.
Look at the sixteen crests of the magnificent Lake Ch'unji.
I tear my life into sixteen pieces
to fly them on the crests.
Fighting this ache of shame,
the day of freedom will come.[10]

In the collections from the 1990s presented here, we find not the combative cries of the freedom fighter, but the beauty of Ko Un's full poetic maturity and that wisdom that needs no explanation, like the "old nettle tree" that guards the village where the poet lives in "Majung Village." With his probing curiosity, he portrays his delight in meeting a kangaroo in the Land Down Under in "Kangaroo"; he gives us the poignant song of the Korean Russians in "Arirang"; and he summons up his memories of how life passes in "Cheju Island."

The power in his words, his imagination and creativity, the magnitude of the struggles he depicts stun the reader. His poems are resonant, limitless. His words are down-to-earth. The imagery is vivid and offbeat. And all of that presents the translators with an almost impossible task.

Clare You

NOTES

1. Allen Ginsberg, foreword to Ko Un, *Beyond Self: 108 Korean Zen Poems,* trans. Young-Moo Kim and Brother Anthony (Berkeley, Calif.: Parallax Press, 1997).

2. Wonhyo (617–686), a Buddhist monk and scholar in the Silla period, was one of the most important figures in the development of Korean Buddhism. He had close ties to the secular world, and his affair with Princess Yosuk produced a son, Sulch'ong, who would

become a statesman and a scholar. Wonhyo's unusual lifestyle made him a romantic hero of novels and poems in later years.

3. "A Dialogue with Ko Un," in *The World of Ko Un's Literature* (Seoul: Changbi Publishers, 1993), p. 22.

4. Ibid. Jun Taeil (1948–1970) fought for workers' rights; his self-immolation was an act of protest against the authorities.

5. Paektu Mountain (literally, "White-Head-Mountain") is a dead volcanic mountain that sits on the border between Korea and China, in the northernmost part of the Korean peninsula; it is the watershed of the Yalu and Tumen Rivers. Paektu Mountain has been the symbol of Korea and the Korean people for many centuries.

6. "A Dialogue with Ko Un," p. 34.

7. Ko Un, Epilogue, in *Songs of Tomorrow* (Seoul: Changbi Publishers, 1992), p. 148.

8. See "Majung Village," p. 29 of the present volume.

9. "A Dialogue with Ko Un," p. 14.

10. Changkun Summit is the highest peak (2,744 m) on the Korean side of Paektu Mountain. Mangch'unhu (2,712 m) is one of the other eight peaks of Paektu Mountain. Lake Ch'unji, the world's highest-altitude crater lake, is located on Paektu Mountain.

The Three Way Tavern

Today

We are alive
as the snow flurries.
Here and there
as our roads change ahead
we are alive.

We used to share the old sayings,
how fresh they are today.
Even for a thousand years,
even for a thousand years,
in the end they're for today.

We are alive
as the snow flurries.
From nowhere
new sounds of a drum thunder.
We are alive.

Let's pick up and leave again.
Cursing the burden,
a pair of shoes over our shoulder,
our flushed faces new to each other.
We can't sink into our graves yet.

Isn't there a place to head for
where the drum beats?
We are alive
as the snow flurries.
We are alive.

Song of That Day

One day I understood
my sadness.
There was no spirit in that time.
I can't stand how
something always
pushes new ideas.

I want to be taken
by the eternal spirit of fiction,
hidden from a mouse or a bird—
spirit solitude
like a kite set loose by children,

to dash headlong in the wind.

Front of a Tree

Look at the man from the back.
If there were a god
would that be how he looked
on earth?

Even a tree
has a front and a back,
not just because of sunlight,
not just because of north and south.
When I meet a tree in front
and part from it behind
I miss it.

Though the tree can't say a word
when it hears of love
its leaves wave in the breeze.
New leaves of a new year
are more freshly green than the old.
No one can stop the turning of leaves
at the end of summer.
No break
between a man and a man
can cut the ties with autumn leaves.
"Stay with us!" they whisper.

The Woman of Kageo Island

Born a man
how could I not have
a most unforgettable place?
There is one such place.

Last summer,
as the winds of Kageo Island in the western sea
tore off my clothes,
at well-side a birch tree stood strong,
wiry trunk
rooted deep as its height,
a *sunbigi* tree stubborn in the wind.

On the memorial day
you can hear the voice of a woman
who gave her man to the sea
long ago,
standing alone with her young children.

Though the winds gust,
her voice carries over,
lightly calling
to her sixteen-year-old son in his fishing boat
across the waves,
not sure
whether it's her son or her dead husband.

Arirang

One day in 1937 Korean men of Yonheju
were dumped onto a cattle train
on a Siberian railroad.
The train chugged along Lake Baikal
pushing forward on a journey of many days
dropping corpses along the way,
one by one, five thousand lives withered away.
Where are we now?
Just reaching the desolate plains of Alma Alta,
cast out into no man's land.
"*Korejtsy,* stay there!"
The empty train left.

Endless folds of snow-capped mountains to the south,
wild fields of weeds front and back,
as we died we started to live,
putting up a hut and hanging a pot.
Sixty damned years're gone,
the second and third generations of
children, Natalia Kim,
Ilyich Park, and
eleven-year-old
Anatoli Kang, who
plays the balalaika beautifully.

As "Arirang" was handed to him
he glanced over the sheet.
Arirang arirang arariyo,
he sang it so well.

Bewilderment! In the child's song
sadness so keen
my eyes welled with tears,
never before had a sadness been so keen.

"Arirang," he'd sung it as never before.
All the ancestors' grief was in it.
Ah, the child's tears,
become one with pain.

Is this song blood or what?
Arirang arirang arariyo.

Grand Dame Choi Kumja

Dame Choi Kumja of Myungpa village,
just below the Cease-fire Line,
excuse me for saying this but,
she's got a big butt in her pantaloons.
Settled in the desolate DMZ,
she walked miles to bring salty water from the sea
to pickle her kimchee cabbage.
Bit by bit she toiled the earth, and
today
her farm grows several bushels of rice.
Now and then strangers drift in.
She serves them a sumptuous meal of fresh farm chicken.
Her husband and sons play second fiddle
to this warrior woman.
Even the sky bows down
for grand dame Choi.

Strange Land

Go!
To a strange land.

Not to America,
not to Indonesia,
away from your daily routine.

Away from the tradition you can't forgive, not even once,
you go!

To the land where babies make up new words,
new words for Grandma, *alupa,*
where even Grandma's
brand new.
Go!
To the strange land.
Forget all your memories and happenstance,
even your empty hands.

Go!
Departure is truly
the new birth
that leaps over your rebirths.
Go!

Cold Mountain

Today I read a couple of Han San's poems.
Han San, he's quite a fella.
He abandoned his real name and
called himself Han San,
after the mountain he climbed up and down.
Quite a fella!

Though he sang of clouds,
of things like wind,
he was no mountain immortal.
He was once a shameless wastrel
deep into whoring.
He couldn't get free,
lost in such things.

He kicked *them* at last, and
panted his way to Han San.
He followed the teaching of Master Majo Doil, then
quit that too for the lowdown beggar's way.
He's quite a fella.
His master?
His mentor?
Is he the fog shrouding the mountain or what?

He's quite a fella.

First

A new chick breaking out of its shell
takes whatever it sees first as its mother.
It could be a crow
      or a crane instead.
It might not be its real mother.

Could our first illusion be mother
      to you and me?

Memorial Night

He had no memory of his dad
who died when he was three,
yet was his dad's spitting image.
His voice changed,
copying his dad to the bone.
When the autumn is astir
he scurries without rest
just like his diligent dad.
On the eve of his father's memorial service
the lamp shines far into the distance.

Song of Innocence

Don't look for the love of innocence in a port.
Ah, not on the streets of neon signs,
nor on the drunken avenues,
you idiot, you idiot,
to look for the love of innocence.

In a time of tear gas and poison gas,
a time of blazes set by flying fire bombs,
don't look for the love of innocence
in broad daylight
or in the early dawn on the deserted streets
            covered with leaflets.

The chill winds whirling through the factory grounds,
they were our salvation.
The cold winds that blew away the dull smog and the sooty smoke
were our salvation.

In a wagon pub on the street
I gulp down two bottles of hard liquor,
drunken brawls were my salvation.
You say not to look for the love of innocence?

The love of innocence? Throw that to the dogs.

Yet, before and after our beautiful thoughts
what a time we had.
Though tired and weak

we had strength to rise up.
Today is another day like that.
After today there is tomorrow,
just that tomorrow's faces will be different.

The love of innocence is there. What joy!

Isn't that
what we are?
When you yelled at us
not to look for love of innocence
in ports
or on streets,
the love of innocence was still there.
Isn't that
what we are?

Kangaroo

When the British landed in Australia
they asked an aborigine,
"What's that thing leaping up and down?"
The native replied,
"I don't know,
Kangaroo, I don't understand you."

The name stuck.

Ah, how much grander not knowing is
than knowing.

A Boat

I keep you there
on the horizon of my heart.
Forever
the boat travels between you and me.

The boat of no return departs.
Of no return,
of no return.

My Resume

From time to time, I dream
after the pelican flies over the Indian Ocean.
Just as my father did home in our village
I dream
in darkness when the light is gone behind the sun.
Awake from the dream
I am alive like the telephone lines whistling in wind.

Until now I fought off dreams;
even in my dreams
I battled to ward off dreams.

Had I known,
I would have cast out
any illusions or
any thoughts that swept by at the time.
What remains remains.

I saw
the phosphorescent glints shining on the sea at night.
I saw
the white teeth of waves
that barely shimmer in the darkness.

What remains just remains.
Like the mother and her baby,
I saw it
shimmering as a phosphorescent light
and gone.

Now I accept dreams,
not only what remains.
I dream
yesterday was
not today,
today is
not tomorrow.
I dream only of tomorrow.

Oh, the good earth is the grave of experiences.

The Cow Is Laughing

Master Lee Yong'ak,
when you were alive,
did you see a cow laughing?
The black cow
of farmer Lee Dukwan
in our village, Hamajung,
kept laughing.
I laughed with it.
Laughing is not a spectator sport
so I laughed my head off with it.
Got on better man to cow
than man to man.
Suddenly
I thought of you,
Master Lee.
How much did you laugh as you left the world behind?

You and I

All those years,
twenty, thirty years.
Conscientious
prisoners in tight cells,
several hundred
aging in the cells.
What are we, then?
What on earth are we, you and I?

Don't even think of good stuff, drinking wine.
What are we?

A Slice of Old Moon

As king I grew thin,
while the people grew fat.
I grew fat,
when the world grew lean.
Always
I watched the waning moon.

Sosan Granny

In Chungnam Province in the Sosan District in the Sosan Township
in a certain village, there was Granny,
seventy and a few more, too.
Home from an outing, her youngest
      grandson piggyback,
she ordered her daughter-in-law, no spring chicken either,
"Come, take your baby,
I must be going now."

The last word trailed out, "go . . . i . . . n . . . g . . ."

Soon she went into her room,
lay down a spell,
and passed on to Nirvana.

Oh, all you Buddhas!
Come bow your heads before her.
Not to Wonhyo,
not to Taego or Bojo or their ilk.
Bow deeply.
Chase away all sorrows.

How lazy is the Sosan drawl!
Before the bleared eye of Granny's life,
burn incense and
bow deeply.

Confucius, One Day

Confucius said,
        I haven't seen a guy who likes to study
        as much as he likes women.
As for me, neither women
nor study,
none of that stuff.
I remembered all the lands of the Warring Time,
the world,
the dizzy world in confusion,
more than the close disciples
whose early death saddened the master,
who ringed around Confucius, or
Confucius, who spoke those words, one day,
he with fastidious taste.
Thanks to him, this far,
and none thereafter.
After Confucius
no one is better than a sparrow.

Majung Village

Over the steep, panting hills where
I rest my heart.
I like the simple homeliness
of the bitch and her puppies.
For how many centuries have
such homely sights been dear to us?
The stern old nettle tree standing by the village gate
gathers sweeping winds.

That's not all.
Beyond the village
the well never dries.
What a wonder it is,
the well's not a dipperful lower.

Children throw stones.
On the other side of the hills
pheasants flutter away, frightened for no reason.

The snow's not gone yet.
An old man, arms akimbo, runs into an eddy of wind.

Ignorant Man

There is a man who knows everything.
He knows everything and says so.
"Yessiree."
How far he is from the sound of the waves.

There is a man who gets it right every time.
He gets it right and says,
"Yessiree."

But, standing over there,
there is an ignorant man.
More things he doesn't know
than things he does.

He's got the same face he was born with,
his daughter is beautiful,
his ancestors rest quietly in their graves.

Empty Field

Don't ask
    why it's so.
Why it's so
    don't ask.
Asking can be foolish.

There are no questions in the sky
    and it stays blue.

The biting cold's gone and
a milky smell is in the air.
For the world
    is coming together,
the thawing earth
    has no questions for the spring haze.

A couple of grandmas come out.
What could they ask each other
    that's new
but to say, here is a green shrub,
here's a potherb!
here is whitlow grass!
shepherd's purse, mother's heart,
pick-purse.
Mustard greens are out.
Oh my, sawthistles!
Here and there
the dusk of early spring evening sets in.

Memories

Tulip yellow blouse,
red skirt,
long braided hair,
a red strip of ribbon
woven in the braid, trails.

One day Father died.
White cotton blouse and skirt,
a white braid-strip.

Ah, the lasting sorrow that
     idles her steps
        soaked in the triple showers.

Where are you now?

My Spring

With the wind that couldn't sleep at midnight
I, too, couldn't sleep. No reason.
It's something so perilous,
I can't touch it with my fingers, but
it comes close to my face.
I can't sleep.
Now the winds are my ideology.

Where were you
last winter?
The spring has busted through my insomnia, and
what do we do
with the flowers on the apricot tree?

In the spring night you can hear horses neighing,
the eggs of this country.
Why is there no answer
to what you hear?

The silence of eggs and egg ghosts!

After Stacking the Chopped Pines

A year after
chopping down the pine tree
it still hasn't died.
Would it say it was on earth once?

As I happened to glimpse the sea
that's what I asked.

In the teeming of waves
in the squawking of seagulls that peck on the waves
nonsense to answer that question.

The Poem in Last Night's Dream

Look at the bird
     at the edge of its nest.
Look at the bird perch at the edge of its nest
     and then fly away.

After the bird has flown
look at the empty nest.
The pure emptiness.
Now look at the gray sky.

In the Woods

In the twilight woods
the child with me
held my hand tightly.
We two as one,
wordless,
walked deep into the woods.

There it was,
my childhood just as I left it,

a single buck loped away.

Mother's Dew

A little baby—
dew formed on Mother's hands—
the baby's forehead got wet.
The little baby
who plays alone over there
wrestles on toiling Mother's back.
For that,
the baby's chest got wet.
I don't want to scrawl on blank paper like this;
I just want to moisten my mind.

Chirping of a Cricket

I heard a cricket stop chirping.
Now after the autumn is gone,
I hear
the life of the cricket
before it came to this world.
No,
its life after this one

at my age of fifty-nine.

A Cup of Green Tea

A bag of young green tea leaves.
And this mature, full taste
brewed from it.

I've been sad poring over that *hwadu* for thirty years.

Grandfather's Advice

Study the mountains,
learn the rivers,
not books on a desk.
Tssk tssk.

Go out and play.
When you're called
at sundown
just answer loudly and come in.
Tssk tssk.

The Road Ahead

Let's not say we've arrived.
Though it's been ten thousand miles,
the road to go is longer
than the road I've come.
Day's end was chancy,
I spent the night like a sleeping beast,
the road to go still lies ahead.
Though loneliness has kept me company,
it wasn't loneliness alone;
it was the world
and the road ahead.
Surely it's
an unknown world.
The wind is rising.

FROM **A Cenotaph** (1997)

My Poems

The 1950s, years of sad zero for me,
rapt drifting,
the full stops scattered here and there after the war
were unexpected salvation.
Because of the magma of the black dot after a word
the words that follow sometimes shone,
making me want to put frequent periods throughout my poems.

As I stepped into the 1970s
my poems
lingered before long roads
like water swirling by the riverbank
that, in a dizzy movement,
flows to the center of the river.
And so
the periods were gone from my poems, and
that salvation grew useless like old shoes.

Poems without periods
didn't end as poems usually do but
flowed on,
on
to other poems.
Searching out the light hidden in darkness,
I could barely see behind the events.

The world's flow
allowed no periods at all
before my poems.
And so
my poems without periods were
destined to move
what I understood,
wheeling from felt soul to felt soul.
Beside that,
everything else I knew
was illusion.

So I dreamed the days,
my poems become other poets' poems,
like flocks of birds flying in,
like flocks of birds landing.
What a sweep of breathtaking movement,
oh, the blue light in dawn!
But today
joins the ceaseless river flow;
my poems will have no periods tomorrow, and the days after

Forgetting

Everyone forgets something.

Forgotten things
from past days pile up,
filling the heart
like useless dust from a mountain range.

Going Over Ssari Hill

Look at the bare tight-lipped mountains,
the village houses barely keep from crashing.
Slanting over Ssari Hill in Muju in North Chulla Province,
the winter sun rushes into darkness.

A few silent passengers
on the local bus.
A young woman
like a half-spent candle
gets tired of holding her cranky baby.

From the edge of Kumsan,
or was it the northern border of the country?
the bus was filled with the baby's cries,
no matter how hard she tried to comfort it.

What could possibly bring such
sadness and suffering to such a young child?
Only the cold lights of Muju on this world, and
no other world exists.

By the Window

What else could I wish for?

There is a faraway place and

a place close at hand.

Sumano Pagoda

Sumano Pagoda
has long stood
in the Chungson Mountain pass in Kangwon Province.
A man dug a pond
in that Chung'am Temple yard in the old pygmy oak grove
and filled it with water
to show his mother the pagoda's reflection.
Actually,
even one Sumano Pagoda
wasn't an easy job.

But this man who had
so little greed
could suddenly see
a silver pagoda,
a golden pagoda in the slanting rays.
What a surprise!

Perhaps he couldn't bear it alone,
so he yelled
to the other men below
"Come up quickly,
come quickly."
Breathless, he pointed
        to the golden and silver pagoda.
The pagoda that stood there
had vanished.
What nonsense!

After the grumbling men had gone
and his heart grew still,
the golden pagoda
stood there again,
the silver pagoda beaming in moonlight.
"Here I am!" the pagoda said.

Fallacy

A certain invisible ray
or ultraviolet light.
Through it
I see your gigantic fallacy shining,
becoming a blossom that invites a butterfly.

Fallacy! What a womb of blessing.

The Poet

For a long time he was a poet.
Children
called him a poet and
women did too.
Surely he was a poet
more than anyone I knew.
Even the pigs and the boars
grunted him poet.

He died returning from a distant land.
In his hut there was not one word of poetry.
Was he a poet who didn't write?
So a poet wrote a poem for him.
As soon as the poem was written,
the wind blew it away.

Then all the poems of the East and the West, old and new,
flew away, swish, swish,
every one followed suit.

Poems of the Peninsula

On the peninsula, we say "birds cry,"
not "birds sing."
Sometimes songs are cries,
other times
piercing cries are songs.
We have to call
even village pigs'
oink-oinks cries.
Of course.
When we slap the new babies' butts,
wa-ah,
wa-ah,
wa-ah,
babies' first cries.
How could they be sad? but still
we say the babies cry.

Spring fades after bursting,
but cold hangs in the air.
In every rice paddy
thousands of frogs croak
all night.
No thoughts,
no feelings,
only the noise of croaking that drowns in itself
all night.

It's summer,
in the heat of the sun.
The cicadas cry
here and there, everywhere all day.
That's the day's
only reason.
If it drizzles
the cries of a wet cuckoo
alone in the rain
fill the valley,
but the cuckoo is nowhere to be seen.

Fall crickets' shrill cries,
already cold in the moonlight,
their cries renewed in darkness
light up the world
in unison.
Is this the moment?
Ah, woman,
are you yourself the spirit of this land?

The frozen silence
of night
tells us winter's here.
Listen in your sleep!
Listen awake to
the cries of wild geese
falling from the deepest well of the sky.

Even the restless angry waves in the heart of the sea,
how not to say the sea is crying?
Even the ridges and ridges of mountains,
the sleepy flags of men fluttering in the sky,
how not to say the winds are crying?
You can't just say the wind's blowing.

We had to cry all together.
"Give it to us!"
All together,
"Give it to us!" we cried out,
hot as molten iron.
Where am I?
Where are you?
We shouted out, banishing lies,
in the thundering beats of the gong,
numbing, dumbing the eardrums.

That couldn't just be us.
As all returned with hoarse voices,
there I was, waiting for you in silence.
After death,
standing again,
there you were, waiting for me.
There you were, gushing out dark blood
again and again.

Then
foolishness merged with understanding.
As the dawn drum started to pound,
we dashed out again, pushing
to stand in the darkness.
Not only the past,
we have to be
the unknown future slanting in.
How can we not be the fresh glittering parade?
The croaking of frogs,
the cries of cicadas,
the chirping of fall crickets, and
all the cries in empty space from earth to sky
where the spirit of geese passes through.

Hometown

Home is a faraway place.
The womb where you rested,
the village where you were born,
the neighborhood where you jumped and played,
those aren't home.

If you go back before you were a man,
that's where your home is.
No, not even there, go back further.

Just try yelling without yearning
in the simple voice of an animal.
What the beast returns to,
the pure land, that's home.

Men won't do anymore.
Animals, mistreated over thousands of years,
transcending greed and foolishness,
are standing up bare in golden sunset.

So nowhere on earth, that's home.

Untitled

Once there was a teacher more than eighty years old.
In his teaching he crossed rivers, forty-nine years
wandering dusty roads in his bare feet.
He talked nonsense
wherever he went.
As the end neared
he pled innocent to his earlier nonsense.
Was it 2,500 years ago?

There was a deaf man who couldn't hear
the teacher's last words.
Forget about the 107 degree heat.
A buzzard hung in the sky,
motionless for a long time,
hungrily ogling
his old carcass.

A Cenotaph

Immortality is so sad.
They raised a cenotaph
in this corrosive world
not to forget him,
never to forget him.
They cut his name
in stone.

Is the wind's glory the wind's alone?
A few ears were put on the stone that
stood firm
in the howling snowstorms.

But the name must not
eclipse the Truth.
How lucky we are who
can't read his name
under the starlight
in the night of wild geese.

The men who gathered once
are gone,
his name faded
from the depth of their hearts.

Immortality is so sad.
In the days ahead, their poor sons
won't remember his name.

The newcomers
will know him even less.

The name on the stone gradually faded.
The ears went dead and
couldn't hear the thunder
rumbling in the storm.

If it's not a name written in storm,
if it's not a name written
far over the ocean waves,
a name that rises quick from the long dead
and carries echoes on the mountain ridges,

then why should his name be immortal
for thousands of years?
The cenotaph is
only a rock covered with lichen,
a stone better buried in dirt
than standing alone.

Anapurna

I go to Anapurna.
One of me who was already there
fifteen thousand years ago
fervently
welcomes the me
who is on my way now.
The two of me collide in a
dazzling destruction.
No word can echo
that dazzling destruction.
I go black there
from stark ignorance under Anapurna.
I no longer exist.
For too long I was a beggar or a lie.

Lullaby

Center the wailing in empty space.
An arrow zings through
      from one side,
shot from the other side.
What the hey!
"Whack," they fall
at my feet
down a thousand miles together.

Baby baby,
sleep well.

The Voice of Baekdam Monastery

As I stepped onto the soil of Inje,
was that his voice I heard?
After Inje and Wontong villages,
walking into Yongdaeri,
was that his voice that I heard?

Closer and closer
to Baekdam Valley in the Surak Mountains,
was that his voice that I heard
swirling in the busy water?

In 1894, he came here as a sixteen-year-old boy,
again in 1904, as a twenty-six-year-old young man,
to save the fallen country, and
to sing.
He wanted to sing,
he wanted to yell
that he wasn't alone.

His words can't be heard anymore
because he's gone?
How can I hear his voice on the wind through the pines?

On the summer night in 1996, you and I and others gathered
in the darkness of Baekdam Monastery.
Did we hear his voice, the words of Manhae, Han Yong-un?

Alone One Day

Today it snowed then stopped.
Dogs romped.
Can I ever stop
        loving the country?
What I crave isn't
the country but
to be free of this love.
The snow is falling again.
I
don't want wine
I don't want books

About the Time Crepe Myrtles Bloomed
—remembering my hungry childhood

About the time crepe myrtles bloomed and
the barley was nearly ripe,
I got so hungry.
The pink bunches of flowers turned a washed golden brown,
I got so hungry.

About the time crepe myrtles withered and
the rice was nearly ripe,
long, long summer,
yet another day,
I got so hungry.

As the pink petals scattered,
dizzily drifting away,
I got so hungry.
Vacantly eyeing the village,
I got so hungry.

But I was told, don't visit the in-laws' house
when the crepe myrtles bloom.
Don't visit Mother's family, I was told,
when the crepe myrtles bloom.
I got so hungry.

Lion

—to Haryong

The winds are blowing.
The winds are blowing
over the Masai Savannah of Tanzania, Africa.
An old lion rests
on a dry grass hill.
Deaf to the winds
he just stares into distance.

Who'd dare make a peep?
Time passes grandly
in his presence,
ripe with no-self.

Winds are blowing.
At last the blazing sun
touches the Masai Savannah horizon.
A silence so deep it calls for friends.

But the old lion just looks.
There's no cause to be dazzled
when the setting sun pierces
his eye.
He lets the sun go bleeding down.

Yesteryear's kings
are mere specks of dust today.
Indifferent to what happens

on the vast savannah,
he just stares into distance.

Large in his life,
he stares into distance
without sadness,
without sadness.
Suddenly he lurches up,
roaring
to the world.
At his roar
all the creatures
in the trees and thickets
fall silent.

Frozen cover of silence—
what's now's tattered rag?

Winds are blowing.
The full moon floats up white
by the lion's tail.
From somewhere
the chirring of insects sounds faintly.
Is it from Kilimanjaro far, far away?

Self-Portrait

The song I sang,
the song I couldn't sing
come crashing down on me.

Is it me?
—running with the torchlight?
Is it me?
—this luminous regret?

Spring News

A distant sound of water.
Deaf
to such noises,
a lump of pork rind hangs
in a butcher shop's red light.
Bewitching, I say!

Sadness

A thinker who's not sad anymore.
No more sadness?
No more sadness?
Who would've thought I'd end up a pauper.

The Winter Sky

What aching blue!

Though it shouts,
nothing can be heard.
What aching blue!
Birds fly away for days.

Breeze

Long forgotten,
long forgotten.
Back to the longing before blaze
rose from charcoal.
Oh, breeze!

Salmon

So sleek and so handsome
she swam away to a distant sea,
with a normal gray back and
a silvery white belly,
lived four glorious years in the sea.

Empty body without food.
Beautiful body,
the head swells,
its mouth hooks,
ugly as can be,
red dots swarming her.

I can't look at
her ugliness.
When the ugly woman
heads straight home
the world lights up.
From far away
you can hear the party drums beat.

Back Home

I came back
to where trash
blooms like flowers—
this is the world I longed for.

I came back
to where hatred
clumps like dry dung—
this is the world I longed for.

Where I spit and swear
at the gray sky,
where the scavengers
and gangs
hustle,
yell all night.

I came back
to where girls giggle,
selling their slovenly bodies
green as turnips,
where no one knows how
to fly a flag high on the pole—
this is the world I longed for.

Passing through a Mountain Village

Passing through,
there was a village
where I wish I was born.
The grace of that mountain village,
charm of her deep silence.
Then I entered a tunnel and
she slipped from my hands.

Okay, I vow to get busy again,
even sweeping the clouds in the sky.

The Croaking of Frogs

The moony night is full
of croaking frogs.
One
frog's croaking

woke up the world
and fused it.

So much for the awakening of Jang Gusung in the ancient Sung.
Where is the croaking
to awaken
all the rest of us?

The masters
were all misers
in their knowing.
All freeloaders on the wisdom
of the frogs.

At Buan Gomso

When I go to Buan Gomso
on a windy day,
the ridges of tide stride up to its court like an old swaying skirt.

There in the court,
I net a few small fish
to eat with my wine.
Ebb tide next morning,
everything's fine there in the court.

My heartburn, is it the lees of the wine?

After a Hangover

Cherry blossoms burst
profusely.
Is regret
only human?
I can't even be a pal to cherry blossoms.
Is regret farther from phony
than remorse?

But

It's been a long time.
I want to write an essay
that begins with "But."

My simple joy
zipped away like an arrow,
destination
unknown.

Where on earth did that arrow land?
That's where
I want to write an essay that begins with "But."

Empty Hands

In the blizzard,
I walked over a little hill
with my wife and daughter next to me,
early morning hours of New Year's Day.
I had wanted too many things until then.
Now I know the bliss of empty hands,
  like fresh clothes that
  make me soar.

FROM **Ten Thousand Lives** (1986–)

Traveler

Why in the world did a traveler come to the servant's room
in this remote village hut?
Jiman, Six-fingers, Cross-eyed, and Lucky welcomed him
to the room, its sooty oil lamp,
walls with bedbug's blood smears like bamboo leaves.
The aimless traveler was delightful as blooming flowers.
Should a guest not be received well, God's punishment would fall on
    the stingy ones.
Poor as they are, they share their kimchee appetizer and cold drink of
    water.
The traveler had drifted here and there,
his stories had no end.
Tired as he was sleepless,
he told stories until dawn.
In the end, as his talk tailed to songs,
he went out to pee—relief, refreshed.
What cries of joy from that sky of stars.

January Full Moon

January full moon, a very cold day,
the wife is busy even before breakfast.
Knowing that the beggars will arrive,
she puts out a bowl of mixed grain rice
and a dish of plantains
on a millstone by the gate of twigs.
At last, an old beggar appears like a whirlwind,
ready to belt his begging song,
but just takes the food and goes away.
Three hundred sixty days like today, and his begging pouch would be full.
After one round of houses, at the village entrance
what joy he feels
meeting another beggar.
No need to go beg at this village, I've already done a round.
Let's celebrate our Dog Moon, he says.
They build a fire with gathered branches
and warm their bodies,
eating lumps of rice out of the bag.
Two beggars with a mouthful of rice laugh and choke.
From nowhere, magpies gather to play up to their friends.

Morning Rooster

At the rooster's second crow, she is thinking more
about her son who left home two years ago
than about her husband who died last year.
Because he's buried
on the hill out back, he didn't leave home forever.
When the rooster crowed at dawn,
Changok was gone, pounding a nail
in his mother's heart.
Hoping against hope he'd return at daybreak,
Mother was up, didn't even have a sip of cold water, just thought of him.
She folded the blankets on the chilly floor of her room,
swept the garden,
swept the first snow fallen outside the gate,
and straightened her back on that thought of her son.

Women of Sunjeri

Deep in the night the dogs in a new town bark loud.
One dog barks, then the next,
until the dog way across the oak hills barks his answer.
In the midst of their barking
bits of words bounce around.
The wild geese fly high in the night sky,
their calls that fall to the icy ground are not strange.
They are friendly calls, ahead and behind, familiar.
When the kimchee cabbages were almost gone in the bean fields,
the women of Sunjeri carried bundles of garlic on their heads to the
    old Kunsan market,
now they're on their way home
after selling off what was left dirt cheap.
The roads run four midnight miles,
three more to go.
The empty baskets are light
but their bellies are lighter without a meal.
This poverty isn't borne alone,
these poor people,
these foolish women, share and share alike.
What a good life they have.
The dogs stop barking
at their familiar voices.
The night's eye glares as if to say, I am the night.

The Street Kids

The street kids ran
down the road to Jung'ttum.
One fell,
burst into screams.
They all took off but
the cry remained,
painful, lonely, an unreasoning rage.
Saburo, that ten-year-old brat.
The brat with the Japanese name, Saburo.

Byong'ogi

Born a hick,
he started working at the age of five,
had to work alongside his dad.
When fall came around,
he went to rice paddies to catch mud snails,
to the wide rice paddies,
as his mom told him to.

It was fun,
half a day hunting snails,
fun to get away from the drudgery.
Byong'ogi,
so good at catching mud snails,
he died drinking lye water by mistake.
No village children knew his grave.
No graves for children, no services for children, just born and died.

Mansooni, Comfort Woman

Though her face was full of freckles
like spilled sesame seeds,
her pretty eyes and eyebrows
swept up in a breeze;
her shadow cast on the water
was an absolute beauty.
She picked castor beans to fill the quota
during the late occupation,
then she was gone, to the comfort unit,
            wearing her rising sun bandana.
Taken by a woman from the patriotic women's association,
she went to earn some money at the warplane-tail assembly plant.
The women left flying the Japanese flag.
At the house of Mansooni
there arrived a coupon for a sack of rice, and
a bottle of fine wine sent by the fawning magistrate.
Ha, what good fortune for the family.
Liberation came, everyone returned,
white bellflowers bloomed and
cicadas sang,
but there was no word of Mansooni.

Letters

When the principal asked his pupils what they wanted to be,
boys wanted to be General Yamamoto Isoroku.
They wanted to be General Nogi.
Girls wanted to be nurses
to care for the wounded at the Battle of Rabaul in the South Pacific.
When he asked me,
I told him I wanted to be Emperor, and
a thunderbolt struck.
"You, scoundrel, want to be Emperor?
How dare you insult our Emperor of the world!
You are dismissed at once!"
My homeroom teacher begged him,
Father followed him home to beg for a reprieve
and got off with three months' suspension instead of dismissal.
Principal asked me again,
I told him a mailman.
I wanted to be a man who delivers messages from one man to another.
I loved the mailman and the mail.
When the mail bike showed up, I closed my books and trotted after it,
though no letters came for me.
Twenty pieces of mail are all the village gets a year.
Anttum Tamok
received the mail by the village entrance,
opened the letters,
used some for toilet paper and folded some for playing cards.
If he didn't get rice cake, he bore a grudge.

He read their mail and laughed at them.
There was no mail for our village, no news
for a while during the Japanese occupation.
No news about life or death
for those away from home.
At last Tamok was caught,
the mailman fired, and
Tamok dragged to court and released after ten days.
I wanted to be the mailman,
but a new mailman came; he had no eyebrows.

Aunt

Aunt of the big house,
surrounded by thorny brambles,
was married off to Hamkyung-do, a distant province.
Just over the hill is far enough but
far away Hamkyung-do,
far away Hamkyung-do.
After she was married off to the nether land,
there was no news but one letter from
far away Hamkyung-do,
far away Hamkyung-do.
When people wanted to know
how many children,
how many boys and girls, Great Aunt had,
she'd answer, one daughter and
two sons.
One is the daughter-in-law to the Lee family
of Solitary Hill,
another is married off to
Hamkyung-do
but she's taken for dead.
As the Harvest Festival came and
the January full moon passed,
Great Aunt never thought of the daughter.
But on her deathbed, she dreamt of her little girl
playing on a seesaw.
She saw her daughter with a scarf and an apron,
soaring high on the seesaw.

Uncle Jaemoon

Clenching his teeth, the old man, half mad after losing his wife in the war,
said,
"Red bastards, red bastards."
Half mad after losing his two sons,
he clenched his teeth again.
As spring followed the cold winter and
the plums bloomed,
he relaxed a little and
drank some wine.
A certain fishwife came along to make a match
with a pretty young thing of Jigong Village
for the price of a rice paddy, the girl was so poor.
He skipped his wedding garb and the bride her wedding gown;
he just took her in as dusk fell.
His wife dead, and
sons dead,
how could this young wife manage the house chores?
The big-eyed young bride was too timid
to go outside
but little by little she dared.
The old man
ogled his bride all day.
Fingering his goatee, he couldn't help but
chuckle and smile.
When the plums flowered, the leaves opened, and
the villagers were famished,

he urged his doting bride,
"Eat more, don't go hungry
though it's old rice,"
as they walked, passing by the graves of his wife and sons.

A Good Day

The day was one in a million,
the clear sky,
clear as the sound of white water.
On a day like this
work gets done with a snap of the fingers.
Things go so easy,
half of the day flies by and
the rest, too.
Blessed with work on this good day,
Sudong's granny and
his mom,
who'd been sour on each other for twenty years,
were suddenly closer than sisters,
growing old together.
The mother-in-law and daughter-in-law went
to harvest sweet potatoes; they dragged the sackful home
and took a break.
The younger peeled a sweet potato,
"Won't you please taste this one?"
"You, go ahead.
I'm not very hungry,
I don't have much appetite."
The dusk was falling.
"We'd better gather the bines."
As the chill set in on their sweating backs,
they were no longer mother-in-law and daughter-in-law
but friends.

Planting Rice

After the cries of the mud hen fade from the rice paddy
the farmers sing at last,
planting rice seedlings.
It's their very own song.
Rich men
A-hem!
live fruitless lives in this world,
never singing a tune.
It's true,
Uncle Dosun
sings our village folk song best,
the lively tune swelling from his throat,
Dosun sings it best.
Just then
the thread on a hexagon spool
rashly unwinds.
Look, the kite's flying away in the sky!

Mountain Well

There'd be no Dragon Village
without the small mountain well.
Large snowflakes fall idly and disappear
in the well's dark water,
no sound, sound, sound
Of all people,
why is the little woman of the Yangsul family
watching the snowflakes melt away?
She went to draw water
with a dipper in hand
and the small water jug on the ground,
no sound, sound, sound

Mitsukoshi Department Store

Third floor of the Mitsukoshi Department Store in Kunsan,
Dad took me there.
I was afraid,
afraid of splendid things,
afraid of Japanese and Koreans.
In the end
Dad and I
were chased out by the saleslady.
She said there was nothing for us to buy there,
said go to the old marketplace,
said go to the new marketplace.
Standing outside the store, looking back at it,
Dad smiled,
"Who wants to go in there, even if they asked us!"
He turned to me,
"Let's go get some stew."
Scary city.
A Japanese boy peered down at me
from a second-story window.
White face,
dressed in a fine suit,
I was afraid of him.
Ttoo—
The port whistle. Scary.
The only things I wasn't scared of,
the bushes, the pine trees,
and our village barkless dogs.

Lark

Soaring
far into the sky,
it drops its quavering song.
Lark!
Aren't you one of our village family?
In the proud green barley field that came through the winter
the village grandpas,
eyes not yet sealed,
watch the world.
Parched world,
cold world,
the world where dogs live better than men
beneath the lark's singing,
the world where beasts come off best.

Kasame Salt Flats

At the mouth of Full View River,
all day long, only two boats go out to sea.
The sea, turned over by the west wind,
breaks into pale distant waves.
On a sunless day
old Jun Jungbae, owner of the salt flats,
stands there
spitting out curses,
Damn it!
Damn it!
All the flats are full of water,
when will they dry and churn out salt rocks?
On his angry face his glasses look even rounder than before.
No, that's not why, not the salt flats, not the salt rocks:
His undisciplined first son
wastes money like water,
he's head over heels in love with Plum Heart at the whorehouse.
Damn him!
I'll kill him.
I'll kill him.

Sudong's Swallows

Only Sudong and his parents live in the house.
The parents leave for work
and Sudong plays alone,
he house-sits his loneliness.
Mechanically he plays by himself with grass leaves
until spring when the swallows return.
Then the new family fills the house.
Sometimes there are bird droppings on Sudong's head
but it's a full, happy household.
Chicks hatch
and grow in no time.
Soon the chicks fly away,
his yard becomes roomier,
he's lonely again.
In late fall, before zooming away
over the mountains, across the ocean,
to head south of the river, to the South Sea,
the sparrows sit on the empty laundry lines
primping their chests.
Watching them,
Sudong matures in his loneliness.
They leave to come back next year.
He bids good-bye to each swallow he named.
Good-bye,
Weet-tim,

Trit-tee,
Weet-ta,
Trit-tom

Ch'ilyong'i

The old man Jaekwon's young hay hand Ch'ilyong'i,
the stripling boy,
walked home,
a big A-frame on his back hanging loose,
fourteen haystacks of hell on it,
with one more on top.
His sweat dripped down.
The master's two cows were waiting for him
to cook their fodder.
Ch'ilyong'i doesn't know his parents,
doesn't know his hometown.
Clear as a bell,
he can hear everything, but he pretends to know nothing.

Chungdu's Mother

Plow day,
the day to hire the plowman to till the farm,
wife of the former district chief,
respected by all in the village, high and low,
she's always warm and unaffected.

Packs lunches for the hired hands,
asking no one for help.
Brings lunch for the farmhands
on her neatly combed head with a disc pad.
She urges them,
please, taste this swordfish,
please, try some instant kimchee.
A good day, full of stars.
In the furrows under the sky,
in the newly turned soil,
the buried worms come crawling out
enjoying the cool breeze.
Her pretty skin under the fine linen blouse
breathes quietly.

Ttaoggi

Rustling leaves nestle around
the house in the sedge grove of Jade Well Valley.
Pretty Ttaoggi lives there.
The frozen rice paddies thaw
in the cast shadow of the facing mountain,
the shadow of the mountain's cherry blossoms.
Pretty Ttaoggi watches,
her dark hair carefully braided by her mom,
dark-haired Ttaoggi.
Her dark blouse with watermelon green skirt can't be slighted,
Ttaoggi always looks bath-fresh.
In this smoothed-over world
she can go alone to gather
such sweet-smelling mugwort.
Ttaoggi, so soft, so pretty.
What thoughts
make her smile to herself?

Tavern Justice

In 1975
South Korea
and North Korea had the same standard of living.
Since then the North has lagged
further and further behind.

Back then, here and there,
back-alley taverns
sprouted on Wonhyo Street of Yongsan in Seoul.

After a few glasses of soju wine
the laborer Cha Dochil blurted
thoughtlessly.

I heard North Korea is not such hell.
The words made him
a suspected spy
and got him sentenced to a year in a cell
for violating the anticommunist law.
The appeals court gave him eight months;
he got out after serving his time.
His future looked bright.
The sun lit
a thousand years of jewels from the Song and Won Dynasties
on the Shinan Sea,
although Park Chung Hee seemed a lot shorter than before.

Three-Headed Eagle

The Three-Headed Eagle
one head looks front,
one head looks back,
the third twists to see
up and down

Soaring high in the sky
he's the guy
he's the guy

spying out the corrupt Chosun bureaucrats,

he swoops down with fierce eyes,
tears the flesh with fierce beak.
Four hundred years of the Chosun Dynasty,
two hundred clean officials,
he picked out the cluster of rotten ones
in the name of the people.

Be proud.
The Three-Headed Eagle will come back
when the people's just wish is buried in the rancor of clouds.

YH Kim Kyungsook

1970—
Jun Taeil dead.

1979—
YH Kim Kyungsook
fell to her death from the besieged
fourth floor of Mapo's Shinmin Party building.

Opened by death
and closed by death.

Kim's grave sits right behind Park Chung Hee's.
Go see it!

Echo

To the mountains at sundown
What are you?

What . . . are . . . you . . . are . . . you . . .

Owl

Owl at noon
can't see a thing
with eyes wide open.
Wait,
your night will surely come!

Baby

Before you were born
before your dad
before your mom

That's when you cooed.

Coming Down the Mountain

I turned around.
Where did it go?
The mountain I just came down?
Where am I?

The old snakeskin rattles in autumn wind.

Bushman

For the African bushman
a dozen words will do
for life.

True Father, Son, and Holy Ghost, the bushman.

Looking Back

Ten years I waited for one snowflake,
my body blazed like charcoal flame,
then burned out.

The cicadas stopped singing, too.

Drunkard

I've never been one guy,
sixty billion cells!
But I get to call the shots.
Sixty billion cells,
all drunk!

Friend

With the dirt you dug,
I made a Buddha.
It rained,
and Buddha turned to mud.

Now what good's the clear sky?

The Three Way Tavern

Wake up,
understanding is a joy.
There can be no sadness,
said the rainy road
when I looked out after three drinks
at the three way tavern.

Late Summer

Jumping into water, splash.
Jumping into fire,
hot!

What a rush, while over there fruits ripen.

Tsetse Fly

A nanosecond,
if that's how long a quark lives,
think about the length of a day.
A day is so short, you say?
You greedy guy.

Moon

Shoot an arrow,
Zing!
The bull's-eye's your eye

The moon rises, sad, dark

Green Frog

Green frog,
because you croaked
the rain clouds massed in the sky.

You sure are a mighty dude,
you little runt!

Held in Your Arms

For a hundred years in your arms
there was no country,
no friends,
no road for me to travel.

Wonder in the darkness!

Cuckoo

Early in the morning, cuckoos sitting in a row,
silent, happy about this world,
and happy about that.
Yesterday's cuckoos gone,
too early to sing today.
Your best time!

Way

This way to Nirvana

Nonsense.
I'll go my way
over the rocks, through the waters,

that's the dead way of my master.

Winds

Don't ask the winds for mercy,
long-legged lilies,
plantain lilies,
tiger lilies.
After all your stems are broken
sprout new buds.

It won't be too late.

Cheju's Reed Field

Cheju's reed field in early November,
a scarecrow propped up
in the whiteness.

He watches the sea; the sea watches him.

Mosquito

Bitten by a mosquito.
Thanks.
Wow, I'm still alive.
Scratch, scratch.

House

Build it high so no devil will know.
Build it deep so no Buddha will know.
Build a house there
and let the white flowers shine at night, creeping along the wall.

Summer

Sunflowers follow the sun without eyes.
Primroses bloom at night without eyes.
Foolish,
dragonflyness by day and beetleness by night,
they know nothing else.

From *A Cenotaph:* Cheju Island

I must go to Cheju Island
not for snake hibernation,
but to be reborn
after snake death.
For my rebirth,
I must go to spirit island.
Once there,
I will fill my heart
with the vast empty stage reaching all four corners of the world.
How can I be born only once?
Many times,
many times over I'll be born.

I was a lonely eagle, hanging in the sky.
I was a nightingale, only able to fly at night.
I was a son of a whore,
who died as a baby,
a big hungry beast,
a pine tree that lost its way
crossing over the beast's back mountain ridges.
And so I may be a far-migrating bird
that can never come down in this world,
a migrating bird that calls
our ancestors' spirits to fly off and away.

I must go to Cheju Island,
the island of so many gods,
tens of thousands of gods
still making sounds of waves.
So many shamans on the island—
old shamans are the rocks laid bare by ebb tides,
young shamans so bewitching that
they can enslave old men.
A red camellia falls
in the night.

That's not all,
sea anemones on the sea floor and
imperishable starfish.
When did Cheju become an island?
It's swung so long as one
with other lands, peninsulas
over the horizon,
chains of islands
secretly connected
place to place in sleep.

And here the mobs of seagulls
follow seagulls already old
who are the sea shamans
that touched down many thousand years ago
to dance their dance of whirling swords,

springing off the crest of waves at daybreak.
At the peak of their soaring
they drop pale liquid shit.
Under the sea the fledglings dance, too,
heads and swords whirling,
spurting from the water,
bright spray of jewels,
in the instant when all the waves begin to dance.

I must go to Cheju Island
to make a great pledge,
greater than any unscrolled in the past,
there, on the island.
I must float a poem on the waves,
there, on the island.
No mission
like summoning the dead man's soul,
sending it off to its final abode
at the heart of the sea.
It's the unknown that can only be grasped by an empty hand.
Waves are dancing.
By the foothills of Cheju Island's Sunrise Hill
the waves dazzle,
dance until they turn to flame.

But it's the wee hours in Shanghai,
I can almost hear Nagasaki boat whistles.
The skies waken on our morning and
their night,
spreading over the oceans.
A restless man appears,
floats a poem across the waves.
Though there's no order in the world,
a noble spirit
surely meets its mate.
The poem floats away on dancing waves
inside a small bamboo tube,
like wine that springs to taste again
after being tightly sealed.
It hears the winds of Cheju Island.
In the sound of winds
there are newborn baby's cries.

The bamboo tube backstroked away.
It left amidst the lovely sounds,
hearing the baby's cry.
It left after hearing the spirited winds
that had blown all month long.
Hey, hey!
what could be more enticing
than comings and goings on the sea?

After a few months, that very bamboo tube
drifted back to shore by Sunrise Hill.
A ghost? Or a dream?
That's how it returned.
I plucked it out like a flapping fish.
There was a new poem in with the old.
What delirious joy!
How long had it been?
How long had it been?

The answering poem said:
  No solitude is solitude.
  If it's true solitude,
  it becomes solidarity.
Floating down with the far current,
washed ashore,
a fresh freedom to welcome with two hands.
What was it?
Eyes glinting in surprise
he opened the bamboo tube.
It was from a poet in Nagasaki.

Twelve months of twirling hats,
that was how the poets
came and went.
There were parties here
and there.

Cheju Island was not alone.
Nagasaki's poems arrived at Cheju Island,
the poems of Cheju's Sunrise Hill
woke up poets in Nagasaki.

I must go to Cheju Island.
There, I'll write a poem,
seal it in a bamboo tube,
throw it in the sea,
standing on a basalt rock gnawed by waves.
The waters take it wholly.
Already the tube has faded out to sea.
Months go by.

Nothing has returned
to where I threw it from.
Days flow by. As I hover around southern Cheju Island,
I see something slapping at the jagged rocks,
the tube!
the tube!
In the very tube I sent away
a poem, not mine,
but about my poem.

The poet who sent it was already dead.
The shamans of Cheju Island knew.
They knew that

leaving this world is
to be reborn in another,
which scintillates with this one.
That's why winds pause and blow again.
The lines of his poem were hastily written:

> As you love women, love birth.

> As you love men, love destruction.

How key
is the foolishness at twilight
perceived and then gone.

I must go to Cheju Island.
The byways of Cheju's seas
were tracked to the horizon and
beyond
by the islanders.
The sea was their rice paddies, farmlands, and roads.
The sea was a secret,
a shimmering code.
Cheju Island exploded the secret.
Then each of its haunts
took a long time to name,

Tough Rock, Tender Sea, Broken Spit
Eyesight's End, Short Cut, Sea Slant Side
Straw Neck, Broken Rope Neck
Broad Yard, named after Broad Rock

at the foothill of Mount Halla and Big Island Sea.
And more, Eyesight Cape with its bounty of edible seaweeds
Blossom Field, Fern Field
where you can eye the distant Fern Field
of Mount Halla,
Front Cape beyond, after passing through Fern Field.
Behind Fern Field, the Banished, and outside of the Banished.
Wide Sea, Sky Wide Sea
Kangnam Sea, beyond which
invisible Eyeo Island
Eyeo Island
Eyeo Island
where life and death are swallowed up.

I must go to Cheju Island.
Not just because
I've roamed the vast waters.
I dream of the vastness
of time,
rushing, heart pounding,
like a first-time thief
to the place where my tube floats off and comes back,
where giddy time expands and swallows ambition.
I must go
for countless slaughtered horses,
for horses the more you kill, the more are reborn,

Jurassic horses already gone,
to meet the shaman of Cheju Island
who knows how many times one must be reborn
in the hide-and-seek, knowing and unknowing,
to be born changed
from the sea floor baring despair
at the sudden loss of ocean,
to fly like an arrow into a new world.

Afterlife

I won't come back as a human.
Ever.

For the afterlife,
an animal will do.
Not a big one;
small will do.
Even
so small it can hardly be seen.
An amoeba will do.

I didn't want that a few years ago.
I could have been reborn
not a man but
an ignorant woman who had lost a few
of her eleven children.
She would do.

But I won't be born as a human being ever again.

Suddenly

Shall we go back
to the songs of the old days,
to the tales of the old, old days?

On a night of blank moon,
well . . .

What a bright moon!
Shall we go back
to those days?

Suddenly, as I squint back,
maybe we've drifted too far down,
wading hither and yon in a lost confusion.

Stars and Flowers

No matter how much
we talk about stars,
they stay
right where they are,
twinkling light
from a billion years away.

And no matter how often
we sing about flowers
our plum blossoms, our childhood,
they don't bloom any longer,
just the usual time,
then blow away
in the first sudden wind.

In this wide, wide world
we excite our hearts,
my stars and your flowers,
old young foolish naivete.

Unlike Laozi

After eating porridge at the Yangzi Delta
Laozi intoned, "Don't go."
The sound of dogs barking
comes and goes.
Had he already arrived in errorless ease?

Night of the moon's long tangled hair

I go further and further
because I like the passing ease so much.

You

When you come and rattle around,
at last I can be me.

When the ice melts and
you're the water,
I become the sound of water.
Next day, when I'm the water,
then you're the purling.

Someday I want to change my clothes with someone,
turning the loud corner of time.
If it's only me, myself, for thousands of years,
what does that mean?
Wherever I go,
it's because of you, you, you, you
that I've lasted so long.

Confession

I don't want to speak.
How can I tell the same story?
Insist on always the same topic?

I fear writing,
sails blown full of arrogance.
How can I write
other stories
on other topics?

Lucky that the sky is so big.
Under that sky,
lucky for the tiny bug.
Neither very big nor very small,
I roam here and there,
using only a few
of the eleven words.

Peace

Most shameful name,
that name,
I write in the sizzling sand of my desert mind.
Peace! it says.
I write it
in the strange script of another time,
long ago,
I write in the sable air of the African earth.

Here
on the peninsular Cease-fire Line,
after the bird has flown,

I caress the helmet that lay rusty all these years,
yearning for
peace!
peace!
on just one leg.

I write "insult!"
standing on my wooden leg.

A Certain Song

The wind blows
all by itself.
You are grass and
I'm a tree.

The winds blow again.
Waves break
over the evening sea.

We keep changing.

Meeting Myself

Slack woods of late November,
so it goes.
Big and small pines, entombed in green needles,
stand quiet to let
everything else
sleep under the sun.
So it goes.
Other trees hang on
to a few leaves.
A bird, finding no place to hide,
flew away yonder
and left one feather.
Suddenly, at the moment's tolling,
I trip on a skull.

Barley Field

Let the South of this land
bear new life
like a barley field in winter.
Like a barley field in early spring
that sprouts, shaking snow off its head.

Be like a keen barley field
that rises up no matter what,
though buried, smothered,
trampled.

Be like a green barley field
that grows stronger
and rises up
when it's trampled.

On the first day of spring,
three green barley plants bring
plenty,
two green barley plants bring enough.
But no barley plants,
what do we do? It's a bad year.

Enduring long poverty
on the hungry barley hill,
the barley is full in April winds.
Like my children,

like my children,
the barley ripens.

Let my golden life be full
like the barley field of the southern peninsula.

Mustard Flowers in April

Late in April
I hurried over to
the northern end of Cheju Island
or before that

The fields of Haenam, Bosung, Gohung
the seaside of South Chulla Province
the mustard fields
there, the breathing sea of flowers

Tipping to the side
falling off
buried deep down
in the deep

Wanted to be a capsized boat
known to no one,
not even myself.

Early Spring

A shy sixteen-year-old boy,
I went on an errand
to the dogless house.

Aunt, newly wed, long teal blue skirt,
smiled brightly,
taking the puppy from my arms.

Though the flowers hadn't bloomed yet,
they were full in my heart with no place to hide.

As I walked back, skirting the wet rice paddies,
my heart had no place to hide,
not even in the boastful puff of clouds.

Searching for the Cow

I went off to find the cow

The branches were webbed with cicada singing.
Without a complaint,
down the rough path
through the thickets,
across the rivers and
over the foothills,
who was looking?

What was he looking for?
Where, oh where, could I hear mooing?

The track

The gurgling of a stream will fade as it reaches the sea,
that dazzling sound.
When I crossed the stream,
I saw the footprints of a cow, and
exulted as though they were my baby's.

Seeing the cow

I saw it.
I saw it.
Like the song of a nightingale, or
a spring breeze,
there was a glimpse of rump.
A cow's rump?
A horse's rump?

You, cow critter!

You critter, your nose has got to be pierced,
so I can pull you.
But you're so stubborn,
uh oh, I'm being dragged away.
One thing's for sure,
there was bad weather between the cow and me.

The cow herder

Though it's tamed by the nose ring and the whip,
he mustn't let the cow out of his sight.
For they're
close heart-mates,
he goads it, git along, git along.

Returning home

He's on his way home,
riding the cow's back.
Yippee kai yay!

Vanished

It's vanished.
It's vanished.
The cow is gone.
The whip and nose ring
left cowless.

After a long nap,
I open and close my empty hands.

All vanished

Neither the cow
nor myself
but a snowflake melted on the brazier.

After returning

Looking back,
I wasted days for nothing.
I wish I'd spent the time
blind, deaf,
letting the flowers bloom and fall.

Getting out one step

I couldn't let it end here, so
I stretched one foot out
into the mud.
The mud bank snickered and said,
"Hey you,
might as well be a bump on a log."

Coda: The Thuja Fence

Because there are few reasons to come and go,
the road is often bare,
like a man after weeping.
Soothing sadness,
the dark blue thuja trees
have shot up since last year and
seem to be hiccupping among themselves.
Some parts of this earth are made
of unfinished business.
So sadness has brought us here, you and I.
Even a man with breathing heels
knows the sun is setting on earth's unfinished work.
The last remaining birds
have flown back to their nests
but their chirping seems to linger
so you hear nothing else.
Whose mind do I have now?
Whose clothes am I wearing?
I am inside the thuja tree fence,
someone outside with whom
I exchanged a few words but
then we stopped talking.
Nothing is wanting,
nothing is wanting,
just the exchange of a few words.
Learning there is no

inside or outside on earth
or the inside and outside are one,
as the naive evening stars
take pity on my body,
I will lean on the thuja fence
and leave the rest to passersby.
We weep together. A guestly turn to darkness.

Notes

p. 8   The Woman of Kageo Island/*sunbigi tree:* A subtropical plant that can withstand strong winds and storms due to its flexibility.

p. 9   Arirang/*"Arirang":* An old folk song with which Korean people like to identify.

p. 11   Grand Dame Choi Kumja/*DMZ:* The Demilitarized Zone along the Cease-fire Line between North and South Korea, created after the Korean War (1950–53) and still a fiercely guarded no-man's-land.

p. 12   Strange Land/*alupa:* "Grandma" in baby talk.

p. 13   Cold Mountain/*Han San (literally, "Cold Mountain"; "Han Shan" in Chinese):* An eccentric, reclusive poet of the Tang Dynasty (618– 906) who lived in caves of the southern and far-eastern mountains of China. His exact dates of birth and death are unknown, but he is thought to have worked during the eighth century. Han San first introduced Sŏn (Chan in Chinese; Zen in Japanese) into poetry.

Majo Doil (707–786; "Mazu Daoyi" in Chinese): Entered the Buddhist community at a young age and became one of the most revered Sŏn masters of the Tang Dynasty. He trained numerous disciples, and his Sŏn style was influential to Korean Sŏn Buddhism. He is credited with the famous Buddhist question "What are you?"

p. 25   Sosan Granny/*Wonhyo (617–686):* A scholar-monk of the Silla Dynasty (668–935) and one of the most important figures in the development of Korean Buddhism.

Taego (1301–1382): A Korean Sŏn monk during the Koryo Dynasty (935–1392) who entered the Buddhist community at an early age, became an influential Sŏn master, and wrote poetry.

Bojo (1158–1210; also known as "Bojo Chinul"): The founder of Chogye Buddhism (named after the monastery he established at Chogye Mountain in Korea). He is known for the dictum *dan-o-jom-su* (sudden enlightenment followed by gradual practice).

p. 39   A Cup of Green Tea/*hwadu (also known as "kongan"; "kungan" in*

Chinese; "koan" in Japanese): A riddle or paradoxical statement used in Sŏn Buddhism as an aid to meditation and a means of gaining spiritual awakening.

p. 50   Sumano Pagoda/*Kangwon Province:* A province on the east coast of the Korean peninsula, with a long, rugged mountain range running through it.

p. 64   The Voice of Baekdam Monastery/*Han Yong-un (1879–1944):* An intellectual patriotic Buddhist monk who fought against corruption in the old Korean government, led the reformation of Korean Buddhism, and then strived for Korean independence after the Japanese annexation. Following a period of detention in a Japanese jail, he spent his years at Baekdam Monastery. His poem "Nim-ui ch'immuk" (Silence of Love) is essential reading for all Korean students. Manhae is his pen name.

p. 67   Lion/*Haryong:* The pen name of Sang-Hwa Lee, wife of Ko Un.

p. 77   The Croaking of Frogs/*Jang Gusung (1092–1159; "Jang Jiucheng" in Chinese):* A Chinese scholar and high government official of the Song Dynasty (960–1279) who wrote a famous poem about the croaking of frogs: "Frog croaking under spring moon/Cracks the poor universe to make one home."

p. 78   At Buan Gomso/*Buan Gomso:* A fishing town on the inlet of the southwestern sea, famous for its fishery products and seaweed as well as its natural scenery.

p. 86   January Full Moon/*Dog Moon:* The last day of November.

p. 91   Mansooni, Comfort Woman/*comfort woman:* During World War II, the Japanese government conscripted young women from Korea, the Philippines, and China to serve Japanese soldiers as sex slaves.

p. 92   Letters/*Yamamoto Isoroku (1884–1943):* A Harvard-educated Japanese admiral who, during World War II, was the chief strategist of the attack on Pearl Harbor.

Nogi Maresuke (1849–1912): The Japanese governor-general of Formosa (Taiwan) during the Japanese occupation of the island.

p. 94   Aunt/*Hamkyung-do:* The remote, northernmost province of Korea.

p. 108   Tavern Justice/*Park Chung Hee (1917–1979):* President of South Korea from 1963 to 1979. Park Chung Hee governed with an iron rule but is credited for the country's economic boom.

p. 109   Three-Headed Eagle/*Chosun Dynasty (1392–1910):* The last kingdom of Korea.

p. 110   YH Kim Kyungsook/*Jun Taeil:* Died by self-immolation in 1970 in protest against the extreme working conditions for teenage laborers employed by garment factories.

          Kim Kyungsook: A women's labor leader who met her death in 1979 during a labor dispute with the YH wig manufacturer when the workers' protest was put down by government riot-control forces.

          Shinmin Party: The opposition party whose building in the city of Mapo was the site of Kim Kyungsook's death.

p. 121   Cheju Island/*Cheju Island:* The southernmost island of Korea, a short distance from the northeast of Japan. A dormant volcanic island, Cheju's old place names were coined after their natural settings (Tough Rock, Tender Sea, Broken Spit, etc.). Numerous horses are raised and killed on Cheju Island for food.

          Eyeo Island: An imaginary paradise Cheju Islanders long to discover.

p. 142   Barley Field/*barley hill:* The period in the spring, around April, when food is scarce.

Designer: Sandy Drooker
Text: 10/16 Minion
Display: Grotesque, Minion
Compositor: BookMatters, Berkeley
Printer and binder: Friesens Corporation